G000123670

Novels for Students, Volume 13

Staff

Editor: Elizabeth Thomason.

Contributing Editors: Anne Marie Hacht, Michael L. LaBlanc, Ira Mark Milne, Jennifer Smith, Carol Ullmann.

Managing Editor, Content: Dwayne D. Hayes.

Managing Editor, Product: David Galens.

Publisher, Literature Product: Mark Scott.

Literature Content Capture: Joyce Nakamura, *Managing Editor*. Sara Constantakis, *Editor*.

Research: Victoria B. Cariappa, *Research Manager*. Sarah Genik, Ron Morelli, Tamara Nott, Tracie A. Richardson, *Research Associates*. Nicodemus Ford, *Research Assistant*.

Permissions: Maria Franklin, *Permissions Manager*. Kim Davis, *Permissions Associate*.

of the publisher and verified to the satisfaction of the publisher will be corrected in future editions.

This publication is a creative work fully protected by all applicable copyright laws, as well as by misappropriation, trade secret, unfair competition, and other applicable laws. The authors and editors of this work have added value to the underlying factual material herein through one or more of the following: unique and original selection, coordination, expression, arrangement, and classification of the information. All rights to this publication will be vigorously defended.

Copyright © 2002
Gale Group
27500 Drake Rd.
Farmington Hills, MI 48331-3535

ISBN 0-7876-4896-5
ISSN 1094-3552

Printed in the United States of America.
10 9 8 7 6 5 4 3 2 1

Vanity Fair

William Thackeray

1847–1848

Introduction

Vanity Fair: A Novel without a Hero, the first major work published by William Thackeray under his own name, was published serially in London in 1847 and 1848. Previously, under various comic pseudonyms (such as Michael Angelo Titmarsh and George Savage Fitzboodle) Thackeray made clear, both in his role as the narrator of *Vanity Fair* and in his private correspondence about the book, that he meant it to be not just entertaining, but instructive. Like all satire, *Vanity Fair* has a mission and a moral. The first published installment had an illustration on its cover of a congregation listening to a preacher; both speaker and listeners were shown with donkey ears. In the pages, Thackeray explains the illustration thus:

> my kind reader will please to remember that these histories ... have "Vanity Fair" for a title and that Vanity Fair is a very vain, wicked, foolish place, full of all sorts of humbugs and falseness and pretentions. And while the moralist who is holding forth on the cover (an accurate portrait of your humble servant) professes to wear neither gown nor bands, but only the very same long-eared livery in which his congregation is arrayed: yet, look you, one is bound to speak the truth as far as one knows it.
>
> That Becky is allowed to live, and to live well, is perfectly consistent with Thackeray's view of life and morality.... Losing is vanity, and winning is vanity.

By the halfway point in its serial publication, Thackeray's long, rambling tale of relentless and corrupt social climbing, told with biting humor and cynicism, was the talk of London. Readers eagerly awaited new episodes in the life of Thackeray's deeply immoral, self-serving anti-heroine, Becky Sharp, who has since become one of the most well-known and most argued-about characters in literature. The novel secured Thackeray's place among the literary giants of his time; and the giants of his time, among them Charles Dickens, the Brontë sisters, Thomas Hardy, and Alfred Tennyson, have endured as giants to this day. *Vanity Fair* is considered a classic of English literature and one of the great works of satire in all history.

Author Biography

William Makepeace Thackeray was born in Calcutta, India, on July 18, 1811, the only child of English parents. His father, Richmond, worked for the East India Company until he died four years after William's birth.

At the age of six, William was sent to a boarding school in England while his mother, Anne Becher Thackeray, remained in India. Unsurprisingly, the young child was lonely and unhappy. In 1819, his mother remarried and returned to England where she and her new husband were able to give him the family life for which he longed.

Thackeray attended Charterhouse School and went on to Cambridge University's Trinity College but did not earn a degree. He studied art in Paris and later illustrated many of his written works, including *Vanity Fair*. It was in Paris that Thackeray met and married Isabella Shawe, an Irish woman. They soon moved back to London where Thackeray launched his writing career. He wrote for magazines, including the famous humor magazine *Punch*.

Isabella Thackeray suffered from mental illness after the birth of the couple's third child. After many failed attempts to cure her, Thackeray was forced, in 1842, to send his wife away to be cared for. Unable to rear his young daughters alone, he was separated from them, as well. The loneliness and separation from family that had been so difficult for Thackeray as a child were no less painful for him as a grown man. Because his wife was alive (in fact, she outlived him by many years) and divorce was not an option, Thackeray never remarried.

The first work Thackeray published under his own name was *Vanity Fair*, a long, sprawling satire that was published in four installments in 1847 and 1848. It remains among his most well-known novels, along with *The Luck of Barry Lyndon: A Romance of the Last Century* (later published as *The Memoirs of Barry Lyndon*) and *The Virginians: A Tale of the Last Century*, inspired by Thackeray's travels in the United States in 1852–1853 and 1855–1856.

Thackeray was prolific, writing short fiction and nonfiction as well as novels. By the end of his life, he had achieved both critical and financial success. In addition, he had the joy of having his mother and two of his daughters living with him and of seeing daughter Anne recognized as a successful writer. Thackeray died at his London home on Christmas Eve in 1863.

Plot Summary

Chapters 1-7

As *Vanity Fair* opens, Amelia Sedley, a conventional girl from a well-to-do family, and Becky Sharp, Sedley's orphaned, penniless, and already corrupt friend, are leaving Miss Pinkerton's school where they have met and become friends. They go to the Sedley home where Becky will be a guest until she goes on to the governess position that Miss Pinkerton has arranged for her.

Becky meets Amelia's older brother, Joseph, called Jos, who is on leave from his government post in India. Although Jos is fat, lazy, conceited, and shy with women, he is also financially well off, and Becky schemes to marry him. Through flattery and false modesty, Becky succeeds in making all the Sedleys believe that she truly is enamored of Jos, and Jos is inclined to propose to her. George Osborne, Amelia's fiancé, intervenes, persuading Jos that he has embarrassed himself in Becky's presence. George does not want a governess for a sister-in-law. Defeated, Becky leaves for the Crawley estate where she is to be governess.

Chapters 8-14

The mean-spirited and stingy Sir Pitt Crawley is the patriarch of Queen's Crawley where Becky takes up her post as governess to his two young daughters, Rosalind and Violet. Sir Pitt also has two much older sons by his first wife. The elder, also named Pitt, is pious and proper to an extreme. The younger, Rawdon, is a dandy and a gambler. The two despise each other.

The irreverent and debt-ridden Reverend Bute Crawley, Sir Pitt's brother, and his nosy, overbearing wife come on the scene. Sir Pitt and Bute also hate each other. The family members are united only in their desire to see their wealthy, old Aunt Matilda dead, and they all connive to inherit her fortune.

George is disrespectful of Amelia in the presence of his army comrades, for which his longtime friend William Dobbin berates him. Physically awkward but highly virtuous, Dobbin has loved Amelia since youth but considers himself unworthy of her. George's father, who has long encouraged George to marry Amelia, now suspects that her family has lost its money and wants George to break the engagement. The self-serving George is willing to do so.

Becky has charmed Aunt Matilda and, at the old lady's request, has moved to her home to nurse her. Rawdon is smitten with Becky and spends as much time with her as he can.

Sir Pitt's wife, Lady Crawley, dies, and immediately Sir Pitt asks Becky to marry him. Here, Becky cries the only genuine tears of her life because she must reject the wealthy Sir Pitt, having secretly married Rawdon. Sir Pitt and old Aunt Matilda are both enraged at this news.

Chapters 15-22

Becky and Rawdon go on a honeymoon, and Mrs. Bute Crawley descends on Aunt Matilda, hoping to turn her against Rawdon and secure her fortune for herself and her husband. Then the Sedleys' possessions are sold at an estate sale; the family's financial ruin, due to Mr. Sedley's unwise business speculation, is complete and public. In the meantime, against the wishes of both their fathers, George and Amelia marry. Next, everyone meets in Brighton where Dobbin announces that the men have been ordered to go to Belgium where the First Duke of Wellington, the British general who is commanding a multinational army, plans to launch an attack on Napoleon's army.

Chapters 23-35

The peace-loving, selfless Dobbin tries to get George's father to accept George's marriage to Amelia, but Mr. Osborne instead disinherits George. George blames Dobbin because it was Dobbin who encouraged him to marry Amelia.

Mrs. Bute Crawley is forced to leave Aunt Matilda when the reverend is injured and needs her at home. Becky and Rawdon then try to move in on the old woman, ostensibly to take over her care, but she is wise to their designs on her money.

Everyone goes to Belgium. The men, except Jos, are in military service; Jos and the women accompany them. George and Becky flirt shamelessly, and Amelia is too blind to understand why she is heartsick. George finally passes Becky a mysterious note and then, remorseful, tries to make up with Amelia.

General and Mrs. O'Dowd, the regiment commander and his wife, prepare for the battle. Mrs. O'Dowd, accustomed to sending her husband into battle, mothers the younger women and pursues her goal of finding a husband for the general's sister. Rawdon is distressed at leaving Becky; George is relieved at leaving Amelia.

The battle begins; the women can hear the cannons booming in the distance. Amelia is worried sick for George while Becky fantasizes about her prospects to better herself if Rawdon is killed. In fact, it is George who dies in the Battle of Waterloo.

Back in England, Sir Pitt has taken up with Miss Horrocks, his butler's daughter, scandalizing the family. Young Pitt courts Lady Jane Sheepshanks, and the sweet, kind Lady Jane in turn wins the affection of Aunt Matilda.

Both Becky and Amelia give birth to sons. Dobbin tries to comfort Amelia as she grieves for George.

Chapters 36-42

Becky and Rawdon manage to live well on

very little money. Becky is an expert at avoiding paying her bills. Rawdon makes a little money gambling. They lease a house from Mr. Raggles, a former servant of the Crawleys but cannot pay the rent. In turn, Raggles is unable to pay his bills and is sent to debtors' prison.

Aunt Matilda dies, young Sir Pitt inherits her wealth, and Becky and Rawdon try to ingratiate themselves with the heir. Becky ignores her son, little Rawdon, but his father loves him. Dobbin gives Amelia much-needed money, saying it was left to her by George. Jos returns to India.

Sir Pitt becomes ill, lingers for a time, and then dies. Young Sir Pitt takes over Queen's Crawley and sends for Becky and Rawdon in a gesture of family unity.

Chapters 43-50

Dobbin is in India with his regiment when he hears a false rumor that Amelia is going to get married. He requests leave to go to England.

Becky and Rawdon go to Queen's Crawley for Christmas where Becky fawns over everyone who has status or money, especially the young Sir Pitt.

The Sedley family is sinking further into poverty. The Osbornes—George's father and sisters —want George's son Georgy to come live with them and offer Amelia money if she will give him up. After some delay, Amelia agrees to this so that Georgy is not reared in poverty.

Lord Steyne, with whom Becky has a vaguely explained and profitable relationship, arranges for Becky to be presented at court—the successful culmination of all her social climbing. She appears draped in expensive jewels; unbeknownst to Rawdon, these are gifts from Lord Steyne. This begins a period of social triumph for Becky.

Chapters 51-56

Lord Steyne sends little Rawdon away to school, which pleases Becky, who cannot be bothered with him. Rawdon, long ignored by his wife, is jailed for failing to pay a debt. Becky is slow to answer his message asking her to have him released so he contacts Sir Pitt and Lady Jane. Lady Jane arrives without delay to free him. At home, Raw-don finds Becky entertaining Lord Steyne. He attacks Lord Steyne—he hurls a diamond pin at his forehead, leaving Lord Steyne scarred—and goes through Becky's belongings and finds her stash of money and jewelry. Both Rawdon and Lord Steyne abandon Becky, and they plan to duel.

Becky pleads with Sir Pitt to help her reconcile with Rawdon, and he agrees to try. Lord Steyne's man, Wenham, uses diplomacy to prevent the duel. Rawdon takes a post on Coventry Island, a remote place from which he sends money for Becky and his son. Sir Pitt and Lady Jane look after little Rawdon.

Chapters 57-67

Dobbin and Jos return to England from India; Dobbin's return has been delayed by a serious illness. Dobbin goes to see Amelia and is relieved to find that she has not married. Finally, he divulges that he has long loved her, but she continues to think only of George. Dobbin spends time with little Georgy and improves the boy's character while Jos belatedly helps his family financially.

Old Mr. Osborne dies, leaving half his money to Georgy and also leaving some money for Amelia. Jos, Amelia, Georgy, and Dobbin go to Europe. Becky, who has been wandering around Europe since losing Rawdon and Lord Steyne, meets up with them and renews her pursuit of Jos. After warning Jos that Becky is dangerous, Dobbin leaves to rejoin his regiment.

Becky reveals to Amelia the contents of the mysterious note that George gave her on the eve of his death at Waterloo: George urged Becky to run away with him. Amelia finally has some understanding of George's true character. She sends for Dobbin, he returns, and they marry immediately.

Becky continues to ensnare Jos and talks him into taking out a life insurance policy with her as beneficiary. Within months, he dies of poisoning. Becky's role in his death is left unclear. Rawdon then dies on Coventry Island of yellow fever. Sir Pitt dies, and little Rawdon inherits Queen's Crawley. Amelia and Dobbin are happy together and have a daughter.

Becky lives comfortably in Europe on the

money from Jos's insurance policy and on an allowance sent to her by her son (who nevertheless refuses to see her). She becomes a churchgoer and gives generously to charity.

Characters

Mrs. Blenkinsop

The Sedleys' housekeeper, Mrs. Blenkinsop is loyal enough to stay with the family when they lose their money. She is also Amelia's trusted confidant.

Miss Briggs

Briggs is at first a maid for Miss Matilda Crawley and later a companion to Becky Sharp. She is good-hearted and naïve enough to loan money to Becky, which Becky, predictably, does not repay. Lord Steyne ends up providing for Miss Briggs.

Frederick Bullock

Frederick, a lawyer, is Maria Osborne's suitor and eventual husband. When Maria's brother George is disinherited, Frederick does not hide his pleasure that Maria is now likely to receive a larger share of the family's money.

Mary Clapp

The daughter of Mr. and Mrs. Clapp, the Sedleys' landlords after they lose their money, Mary becomes Amelia's friend.

Mr. Clapp

Mr. Clapp is the Sedleys' longtime clerk, who takes the family in when they lose their fortune.

Mrs. Clapp

The Sedleys' landlady, Mrs. Clapp, nags Amelia about the rent when the family has fallen on hard times, but she changes her attitude when Amelia comes into money.

Bute Crawley

The brother of Sir Pitt Crawley, Bute is a reverend who is ill-suited to his position. He likes to eat, drink, and gamble (and therefore is in debt) and is happy to let his wife run their household and write his sermons. Like all the Crawleys, he hopes to inherit a substantial amount of money from old Aunt Matilda Crawley.

Mrs. Bute Crawley

The reverend's wife is overbearing, snooty, manipulative, and determined to win Aunt Matilda's fortune. She dislikes Becky Sharp, whom she recognizes as a smart and ambitious competitor. In the end, Mrs. Crawley fails to secure Aunt Matilda's money.

James Crawley

The son of Bute and Mrs. Crawley, James nearly charms Aunt Matilda into leaving him her money. When she discovers that he is a heavy drinker and catches him smoking in her house, he falls from grace and loses his chance at the inheritance.

Miss Matilda Crawley

Miss Crawley, Sir Pitt Crawley's half-sister, is old, unmarried, eccentric, and rich. The entire Crawley clan connives to get their hands on her fortune, and she is well aware of this. She is at first inclined to favor Rawdon, but he loses out when he marries Becky; Miss Crawley disapproves of the union because of Becky's low social standing. Although she dislikes Pitt (mostly for his extreme piety), in the end, Pitt's wife, Lady Jane, wins the old lady's affection through genuine kindness, and Pitt and Lady Jane end up with most of Miss Crawley's fortune.

Pitt Crawley

Pitt is the older son of Sir Pitt Crawley. He is overly pious, proper to a fault, and stingy. It is mostly due to his marriage to the sweet and kind Lady Jane that Pitt ends up with his aunt's fortune. His seat in Parliament is also inherited, and not won by any personal merit. However, Pitt does have some redeeming qualities. He welcomes Rawdon and Becky into the family, and when they split up, Pitt offers his brother kindness and takes care of their son (also named Rawdon).

Sir Pitt Crawley

Sir Pitt is a wealthy nobleman who is nevertheless uneducated, unrefined, unkempt, uncouth, and a penny pincher in the extreme. He has two sons, Pitt and Rawdon, by his deceased first wife, and two young daughters, Rosalind and Violet, by his second wife, Rose. Becky comes to his country estate, Queen's Crawley, to be governess to his girls. When Rose dies, Sir Pitt proposes to Becky (he likes her spunk), who must refuse him because she has secretly married Rawdon. Sir Pitt then turns his affections to his butler's daughter, Miss Horrocks, which horrifies his family. He dies and leaves his fortune, along with his noble title of baronet, to his elder son, Pitt.

Rawdon Crawley

Rawdon is the younger son of Sir Pitt Crawley and, eventually, the husband of Becky Sharp. When he is kicked out of Cambridge University, his aunt, Miss Matilda Crawley, who favors him until he marries Becky, buys him a commission in the Life Guards Green. Although somewhat dull-witted himself, Rawdon is a gambler who takes advantage of less clever men whenever he can and helps support himself and Becky in this way. He truly loves Becky and puts up with her increasing neglect and disregard for him. It is too much for him, however, when he is imprisoned for debt, and it is

Lady Jane, not Becky, who comes to free him. Rawdon goes home to find Becky with Lord Steyne and finally leaves her. He takes a position on a faraway tropical island, Coventry Island, from which he sends money for Becky and their son. Eventually, he dies of yellow fever on the island.

Rawdy Crawley

Rawdy is the son of Becky and Rawdon. Although his father loves him, Becky shows no love or affection for him and sends him away to school under the auspices of Lord Steyne. Pitt and Lady Jane take care of him after his parents part ways, and Rawdy inherits Queen's Crawley when Pitt dies. Although he will not see her, he provides for Becky in spite of her ill treatment of him.

Miss Rosalind Crawley

Rosalind is the daughter of Sir Pitt by his second wife and Becky's charge when Becky comes to Queen's Crawley.

Miss Violet Crawley

Violet is the daughter of Sir Pitt by his second wife and Becky's charge when Becky comes to Queen's Crawley.

William Dobbin

Dobbin is the only truly noble character in

Vanity Fair. He has few outward virtues—he is awkward and unattractive—and has little money; but he is selfless, loyal, kind, truthful, and generous. He spends his life providing support and service to undeserving and ungrateful friends, among whom the closest are George Osborne and Amelia Sedley. Although Dobbin loves Amelia, he feels that he is not a good enough match for her and so goes out of his way to ensure that George marries her. His dogged devotion to Amelia is finally rewarded when Amelia marries him long after George has died. In the end, however, Dobbin realizes that Amelia was never worthy of him or of the kind of love he has shown her.

Horrocks

Horrocks is Sir Pitt's butler.

John

The Sedley's groom, John drives Becky to Sir Pitt's home after her visit with the Sedleys. John is rude to Becky, chiefly because Amelia has given her some clothes that John hoped to have for his girlfriend.

Media Adaptations

- Unabridged audio versions of *Vanity Fair* have been published by Audiobook Contractors (1987), Books on Tape, Inc. (1989), and Black-stone Audio Books (1999, in two parts, with Frederick Davidson as the reader). Abridged versions have been published by Highbridge Co. (1997, with Timothy West as the reader), Naxos Audio Books (1997, with Jane Lapotaire as the reader), and HarperCollins (1999, with Miriam Margolyes as the reader).

- Films were made of *Vanity Fair* in 1911, 1915, 1922, 1923, 1932. The 1932 movie was directed by Chester M. Franklin, written by F. Hugh Herbert, and starred Myrna Loy as

Becky Sharp. A new film is in production with Janette Day as the producer and scriptwriters Matthew Faulk and Mark Street.

- *Vanity Fair* was made into a television minis-eries in 1971, 1987, and 1998. The 1971 version, directed by David Giles III and written by Rex Tucker, is available on videotape. The 1987 version was directed by Diarmuid Lawrence and Michael Owen Morris and written by Alexander Baron. The 1998 version was directed by Marc Munden and written by Andrew Davies, and starred Natasha Little as Becky Sharp. It also is available on videotape.

Glorvina Mahoney

Peggy O'Dowd's flirtatious sister, Glorvina pursues William Dobbin, who is too fixated on Amelia to show any interest.

Colonel Michael O'Dowd

The Colonel is George Osborne and William Dobbin's commanding officer, a brave, experienced soldier who becomes a major general. He has an amiable relationship with his wife.

Peggy O'Dowd

The Colonel's wife is Irish, talkative, and genuinely kind. Her primary goal is to make a match for her sister, Glorvina.

George Osborne

George has longstanding relationships with the Sedley family and with Dobbin. He is a goodlooking, self-centered, prideful, free-spending, gambler. He has a certain amount of wealth but not nobility, and he courts the favor of all aristocrats who cross his path. It is George who ruins Becky's hopes of marrying Joseph Sedley by convincing Joseph that it would be inappropriate for him to marry a governess. George does this not out of concern for Joseph but because he is engaged to marry Joseph's sister, Amelia, and does not want a governess in the family.

While Amelia loves George, George is incapable of loving anyone as much as he loves himself. He nearly backs out of marrying Amelia (his father is against the union and in fact disinherits George over it), but Dobbin persuades him to go through with it. Then, just before going off to the Battle of Waterloo, George flirts with Becky and passes her a mysterious note. George is killed in the battle, and Amelia grieves deeply. She doesn't find out until many years later that George's note to Becky suggested that the two of them run away together.

Georgy Osborne

Georgy is the son of George and Amelia. His father dies before he is born. Although he is spoiled by his mother and seems destined to grow up to be even more selfish and vain than his father, Dobbin influences him for the better. His grandfather leaves Georgy half the family fortune, in spite of having disinherited his father, George, over George's marriage to Amelia.

Jane Osborne

One of George's sisters, Jane is a lonely, unmarried woman whose life is considerably uplifted when young Georgy comes to live at the Osborne family home.

Old John Osborne

Father of George, John is a mean, calculating, unforgiving man. He has encouraged George to love and marry Amelia throughout his son's youth, but when the Sedley family loses its fortune, John orders George to give Amelia up. When George refuses, John disowns and disinherits him and refuses to have anything to do with Amelia. After George's death, the old man remains hard toward Amelia but wants to rear his grandson, to which Amelia finally agrees. In part because of Dobbin's efforts, John mellows somewhat in his old age. He comes to love Georgy and not only leaves a substantial amount of money to his grandson, but also provides for Amelia.

Maria Osborne

One of John Osborne's three daughters, Maria is rather like her father. She welcomes her brother's disinheritance because it means more of the family fortune for her, and she marries a lawyer who is equally cold and calculating. When her father leaves Georgy and Amelia money, Maria plots to have one of her daughters marry Georgy so that she can control more of the family money.

Miss Barbara Pinkerton

Miss Pinkerton owns the academy where Amelia Sedley and Becky Sharp meet and become friends. Miss Pinkerton dotes on Amelia because her family has money and hates Becky as much for her poverty as for her churlish attitude.

Charles Raggles

Raggles works as a gardener for the Crawleys and saves his money until he is able to buy a greengrocer shop and house of his own. Becky and Rawdon come to be his tenants but do not pay their rent. They cheat him until finally they have ruined him, and Raggles ends up in debtors' prison.

Amelia Sedley

Amelia is the daughter of John Sedley, a

businessman who is successful and moneyed as the novel opens. She is sweet, kind, malleable, naïve, and shallow.

Amelia's love for George Osborne is blind love. On the eve of the Battle of Waterloo, as George flirts with Becky, Amelia is deeply distraught at George's imminent departure for the battle. George is handsome, and Amelia doesn't see beneath the surface to the ugliness underneath, any more than she sees the nobility beneath Dobbin's unattractive appearance. Even after George's death, she remains as unaware of his lack of integrity and devotion as she is of William Dobbin's love for her.

Amelia is a loving mother to Georgy, the son born to her after George's death. She finally marries Dobbin but only after Becky awakens her to his virtue.

John Sedley

Father of Amelia and Joseph, John Sedley is, when the novel begins, a well-to-do merchant and a friend of John Osborne. Sedley is amenable to Becky's plot to marry Joseph, as he fears that the alternative will be an Indian woman; Joseph is on leave from his government post in India. Sedley takes unwise business risks in an effort to increase his wealth but instead loses everything. The family is forced to rent a lowly cottage owned by one of their former servants. Sedley then spends his time concocting schemes to regain his wealth, but he dies penniless.

Mrs. John Sedley

John Sedley's wife is sweet-tempered and loyal like her daughter, Amelia, but her good nature gradually is ground down by the family's ongoing poverty. Amelia takes care of her during her last illness.

Joseph Sedley

Joseph is Amelia's older brother. He loves nothing more than food, drink, and sleep. His father tells his mother, "if you and I and his sister were to die tomorrow, he would say, 'Good Gad!' and eat his dinner just as well as usual." He is fat and cowardly, yet conceited and a dandy. At Waterloo, he goes no nearer the battlefield than the women do and still shakes with fear, and yet he later tells such tales of his courage that he is given the nickname "Waterloo Sedley." He believes that Becky is genuinely attracted to him, when her only real interest is in his money, and plans to propose to her until George dissuades him. When his father goes bankrupt, Joseph sends only a little money and is tardy even with that.

Joseph meets Becky in Europe after her husband has left her, and she charms him just as she had years earlier. Joseph and Becky travel together, but Joseph confides to Dobbin that he is frightened of Becky. Joseph soon dies of poisoning, and it is left unclear whether Becky has murdered him for his only remaining asset, an insurance policy whose proceeds are split between Becky and Amelia.

Becky Sharp

See Rebecca Sharp

Rebecca Sharp

Becky Sharp is the central character in *Vanity Fair* and Amelia Sedley's opposite. She is the orphaned daughter of destitute parents, and she learns early on to look after her own interests in all situations. Becky values money and social status above all and is thoroughly corrupt in her pursuit of them. Her most well-known (though often doubted) observation is that for five thousand pounds a year, she could be a good woman. Selfish, unscrupulous, manipulative, and ambitious, she is capable of appearing sweet, mild, and even timid when it furthers her aims to do so. She can blush and cry at will but cries genuinely only once: when she is forced to turn down the wealthy Sir Pitt's marriage proposal because she has already secretly married his son.

Becky is helped in her relentless social climbing both by her wits, which are as keenly honed as her surname implies, and by her physical attributes, which are listed thus: "Green eyes, fair skin, pretty figure, famous frontal development." Nearly all the male characters in the novel are taken in by her, always to their detriment.

As the novel opens, Becky attends Miss Pinkerton's academy where she earns her keep by teaching French (learned from her mother). She becomes Amelia's friend and goes to her home for a long visit when the two leave the academy. There she tries to lure Amelia's brother Joseph into marrying her but is foiled by George Osborne. She then goes to work as a governess for Sir Pitt Crawley and marries his son Rawdon, a marriage that gives her status but not wealth. In a series of attempts to secure money, she sacrifices her marriage and ignores her child. Her vaguely defined relationship with Lord Steyne provides both money and position until Rawdon walks in on them and both men abandon her.

In the end, Becky has attained a measure of middle-class respectability—the place in Vanity Fair that she has so long and so ardently sought. Her status is made possible partly by money inherited from Joseph Sedley, whom she meets again after many years and whose death by poisoning she may have caused.

Becky's corruption does not render her incapable of recognizing or appreciating virtue in others, even though virtue is rare in Vanity Fair. She is able to see the noble character of William Dobbin and, in an unexpected act of caring, helps Amelia to see it too, so that Amelia will marry Dobbin.

Lord Steyne

Lord Steyne is a wealthy aristocrat and lord of the Powder Closet at Buckingham Palace. He is unattractive in every conceivable way and considerably older than Becky, but she enters into a vague arrangement with him that earns her money, jewelry, and status until her husband walks in on Becky and him and throws a brooch at Lord Steyne, scarring him for life.

The Marchioness of Steyne

Lord Steyne's wife is a good woman, reduced to silence and superstitious religiosity by her husband's degeneracy. She comes to Becky's defense after Rawdon wounds Lord Steyne and both men desert her.

Wenham

Wenham is Lord Steyne's servant. He prevents Lord Steyne from dueling with Rawdon over Becky and turns Sir Pitt against Becky.

Themes

Vanity

There is one clear, overarching theme in *Vanity Fair: A Novel without a Hero*, and Thackeray telegraphs it in his title and subtitle. In the pages of *Vanity Fair*, all is vanity and all are vain. Some are more vain—more obsessed with self and with the ephemeral treasures of social position and money—than others, but none, in the author's estimation, can be called heroic.

The title is borrowed from John Bunyan's *The Pilgrim's Progress*, in which Vanity Fair is a town that exists for the purpose of diverting men and women from the road to heaven. The town's residents are all mean and ignorant, and they all make their living by enticing passersby to spend what they have on worldly vanities—items that offer brief sensual pleasure but have no lasting value. Thackeray transports Vanity Fair to London in the early 1800s and peoples his version with characters, primarily from the middle and upper classes, who live only to obtain higher social status and more money, and who are happy to lie, cheat, steal, manipulate, and betray in the pursuit of these goals. It is worth noting, as well, that Thackeray's Vanity Fair, like Bunyan's, is explicitly a godless place; both authors believe that the unrestrained vanity they portray is possible only among people who have no concept of a God who sets, upholds, and enforces moral standards. In an often-quoted letter to a personal correspondent, written in July 1847, before *Vanity Fair* was finished, Thackeray wrote, "What I want is to make a set of people living without God in the world ... greedy, pompous, mean, perfectly self-satisfied for the most part and at ease about their superior virtue."

Topics for Further Study

- Do some research on Thackeray's life. Write an essay exploring some ways in which the author's life experiences are reflected in the characters and the story of *Vanity Fair*.

- Compare and contrast Becky Sharp and Amelia Sedley. Consider each woman's background, personality, values, strengths and weaknesses, and fate. What, if any, similarities do they share? What elements do you find that point to why they each turned out as they did?

- Imagine that you are Miss Matilda Crawley. Write your last will and testament, telling to whom you are leaving your fortune and why.

- Research the Battle of Waterloo. Give some possible reasons for Thackeray's having included it as a setting in the novel. Why is this battle a fitting background for these characters and their story?

- How is the society in which you live similar to the one depicted in *Vanity Fair*, and how is it different? Present your answer in any form you choose, such as an essay, short story, or poem.

Thackeray succeeded so well in doing this that the novel has been faulted, more often than for anything else, for the unrelenting baseness of its characters. The vainest of all is Becky Sharp. Becky is proud of the physical attractiveness and clever wit that allow her to charm men. Her ultimate effect on them is similar to a spider's effect on a fly, which finds itself trapped and consumed. As her first husband, Rawdon Crawley, goes off to the Bat of Waterloo, Becky muses that she will be free to marry a wealthier man if Rawdon is killed. When he is not killed, Becky makes the best of it, using his aristocratic pedigree to win entrance to the social circles she seeks and to help her avoid paying her bills. Meanwhile, she uses other men, especially Lord Steyne, to get what she cannot get from her husband (money), carrying on public relationships that humiliate him, and ignoring him and their son. After Rawdon has finally left her for a faraway island, where he dies of a tropical disease, Joseph Sedley has the bad luck to encounter Becky a second time, and the drama of the spider and the fly again unfolds. Becky seduces Joseph and soon talks him into taking out a life insurance policy with her as beneficiary. Within months, Joseph is dead of poison; whether by Becky's hand or not is left to the reader to decide. There is scant evidence in the novel that murder would be beyond her.

Most of those around Becky are not better than she is, they are simply less clever and less desperate. Joseph is lazy, gluttonous, dull, and uncaring. When his father goes bankrupt and his whole family is on the verge of starvation, he doesn't get around to sending relief until it is nearly too late. George Osborne, Amelia's husband, is unable to love anyone but himself. George's father is mean, calculating, and unforgiving. Old Sir Pitt is a vulgar skinflint. Reverend Bute Crawley is not at all reverent and lets his overbearing gossip of a wife write his sermons. The list goes on and on.

Among the main characters, only Amelia Sedley and William Dobbin approach virtue.

Amelia's fault is not so much that she is vain as that she is too blind and too shallow to recognize either vanity or virtue even at point-blank range. She idolizes George, the self-absorbed cad; she fails to see that Dobbin is a better man by far, even after years of his selfless attention to her. And Amelia is not completely above vanity. She is self-centered enough to accept Dobbin's devotion and his generous gifts without thinking of his feelings and without even expressing much gratitude.

Dobbin alone possesses real integrity and moral maturity, but even he is tinged with vanity. He is selfless, loyal, generous, and kind, ever content to give more than he takes. Dobbin's failure, similar to Amelia's, is his lack of discrimination about the characters of those around him. As a result, he gives people much more and much better than they deserve; in other words, he spends his life casting pearls before swine. And Dobbin's vanity lies in his dogged devotion to Amelia, who is, like the wares hawked at Bunyan's Vanity Fair, glittery but not golden. She is not a heroine, worthy of a hero; she is just a generally decent, conventional, sweet-tempered woman. Though he does finally realize that Amelia has not been worthy of the adoration he has heaped on her, as a character, Dobbin is weakened by the fact that it takes him half a lifetime to develop a realistic view of Amelia.

Style

Victorian Literature

It was during the Victorian period (1837–1901) that the novel became the dominant literary form. *Vanity Fair* is considered one of the classic novels of the era. It was common for novels to be published serially, in magazines or in stand-alone sections. *Vanity Fair* was first published serially, and the early parts were published before the later ones were written. This at least partly explains the novel's many irregularities. A character may be called by different names in different sections (Mrs. Bute Crawley may be Barbara or Martha; Glorvina may be Glorvina Mahoney, the sister of Mrs. O'Dowd, or Glorvina O'Dowd, the sister of the general). One name may also be shared by multiple minor characters, and both the narrative and the passage of time may jump and start in unexpected directions. In one particularly confusing instance, Thackeray relates the details of Joseph's visit to his family and then has Amelia receive a letter from Joseph informing her that his visit will be delayed. To put it simply, Thackeray made it up as he went along, without undue concern for consistency. The novel's generous length and enormous cast of characters are also characteristic of the time.

Thackeray and Charles Dickens were the leading lights in Victorian fiction, constantly compared and always uncomfortable around each other. Dickens was born a year after Thackeray but was well established by the time Thackeray began to attract notice. Thackeray's focus was on the middle and upper classes, while Dickens's was on the poor. Thackeray's works, including *Vanity Fair*, are considered less sentimental and more subtle than Dickens's.

Loose Structure

Vanity Fair is not only long, it is meandering. Thackeray knows where he is taking his readers, but he is in no hurry to get them to their destina. Any slight forward movement of the plot may cause the author to stop, reflect, pontificate, digress. There are many long essays on everything from how to live with no visible means to how women treat one another. Other topics include how people comport themselves at estate sales, what the relationships between servants and employers are like, and what types of wedding and funeral ceremonies are practiced. Thackeray addresses readers directly, sometimes telling them what they can expect in the coming pages, sometimes telling them what to think of a character, and sometimes sharing his own musings and desires (one of which is for a rich, old aunt like Miss Matilda Crawley).

Many characters, including minor ones, also are given space to express their perspectives on other characters, story events, settings, and life in general. The story is told primarily from the point of view of a single narrator, but this narrator is often interrupted by story characters and by the author himself.

Thackeray's wanderings cover more than just philosophical terrain. Readers follow various characters all over England and to Brussels, Paris, Rome, the comically named, fictional German principality of Pumpernickel, and India, as well as to the British royal court and to an infamous debtors' prison.

Satire

Above all else, *Vanity Fair* is a satire. *The Penguin Dictionary of Literary Terms and Literary Theory* cites Thackeray among the principal satirists of the nineteenth century and *Vanity Fair* as a key work. It defines satire by defining its author:

> The satirist is ... a kind of self-appointed guardian of standards, ideals, and truth; of moral as well as aesthetic values. He is a man (women satirists are very rare) who takes it upon himself to correct, censure, and ridicule the follies and vices of society and thus to bring contempt and derision upon aberrations from a desirable and civilized norm. Thus satire is a kind of protest, a sublimation and refinement of anger and indignation.

As much as *Vanity Fair* meanders in terms of

content, it remains steadfastly on point when it comes to tone; it is satirical from start to finish, and all characters, even the few virtuous ones, take their share of darts. The sharpest arrows, though, are aimed at the worst of the lot. When the ignorant, vulgar tightwad Sir Pitt proposes to Becky, he makes a tall tale of a speech that makes him out as a generous gentleman whose only fault might be his advanced age. He tells Becky:

> "I'm an old man, but a good'n. I'm good for twenty years. I'll make you happy, zee if I don't. You shall do what you like; spend what you like; and 'av it all your own way. I'll make you a zettlement. I'll do everything reglar. Look year!" And the old man fell down on his knees and leered at her like a satyr.

The humor is compounded when Becky responds with equal corruption. Although she is distraught only because she is already married to Sir Pitt's much less wealthy son, she does a good job of acting as if she believes Sir Pitt to be the prize of manhood and explaining that that is why she is in tears at having to turn him down.

Virtually every character in the book, starting with Becky Sharp, is satirized every time his or her connotation-laden name is mentioned. But the most obvious and outrageous names are saved for minor characters: the auctioneer is Mr. Hammerdown; the surgeon, Dr. Lance; the hanging judge, Sir Thomas Coffin; the gambler, Deuceace, to give a very few examples. Also on Becky's rain-drenched trip to Queen's Crawley, she passes the towns of Leakington, Mudbury, and Squashmore.

Thackeray's satire often takes the form of irony (figurative speech in which what is meant is the opposite of what is said). People who hate each other address each other as "my love." The degenerate Lord Steyne calls his house a "temple of virtue" and describes his long-suffering and pious wife as being as gay as Lady MacBeth. Of the warbeleaguered Belgians, the author writes, "For a long period of history they have let other people fight there."

Wide-Ranging Allusions

It would take a lifetime study of world literature and history to comprehend every allusion in *Vanity Fair*. References to Greek and Roman classics and the Bible are not unexpected. But Thackeray adds dozens of references much more obscure to modern Western readers. To name just a few: Ahriman, a Zoroastrian evil spirit; the Arabian nights; and a French opera performed in London at the time Thackeray was writing. His several allusions appear as represented in the following passage:

> 'Come, come,' said James, putting his hand to his nose and winking at his cousin with a pair of vinous eyes, 'no jokes, old boy; no trying it on on me. You want to trot me out, but it's no

go. In vino veritas, old boy. Mars, Bacchus, Apollo virorum, hay? I wish my aunt would send down some of this to the governor; it's a precious good tap.'

James is quoting (not accurately) the *Latin Grammar* he studied at school; the main gist is "truth in wine." "Machiavel" is Thackeray's short form of Machiavelli and the author's nickname for Sir Pitt.

Napoleon and the Battle of Waterloo

The Napoleonic Wars began in the late 1790s, with Napoleon Bonaparte leading the revolutionary government in France. For the next several years, the British suffered military defeats at sea, several attempted invasions by the French, as well as the economic inflation and disruption that often accompany war. The British formed a series of alliances to fight the French, and the Fourth Coalition, comprising Britain, Russia, Prussia, and Austria, succeeded in routing Napoleon and exiling him in 1814. In 1815, Napoleon escaped from exile on the island of Elba and retook the French throne. It is this event that brings the major characters of *Vanity Fair* to Brussels and leads to the famous Battle of Waterloo.

At the news of Napoleon's return, the Fourth Coalition nations quickly committed a force of 150,000 soldiers to gather in Belgium and invade France on July 1, 1815. The British general, Arthur Wellesley, the First Duke of Wellington, was the chief commander of the coalition force. Napoleon responded by planning a secretive, preemptive strike against the assembling troops. He reached the Belgian border on June 14, with nearly 125,000 troops, and crossed it on June 15.

With the advantage of surprise, Napoleon succeeded in splitting the two sections of the coalition force and thus held the strategic upper hand. Four days of fierce fighting and desperate strategizing on both sides followed, culminating at Waterloo on June 18. On that day alone, 40,000 French soldiers and 22,000 coalition soldiers were killed; Waterloo was one of the bloodiest battles of modern times. Here is Thackeray's description:

> All day long, whilst the women were praying ten miles away, the lines of the dauntless English infantry were receiving and repelling the furious charges of French horsemen. Guns which were heard at Brussels were ploughing up their ranks, and comrades falling, and the resolute survivors closing in. Towards evening, the attack slackened in its fury. They ... were preparing for a final onset. It came at last: the columns of the Imperial Guard marched up the hill of Saint Jean.... It seemed almost to crest the eminence, when it began to wave and falter. Then it stopped, still facing the shot. Then at last the English troops rushed from the post from which no enemy had been able to dislodge them, and the Guard turned and fled.
>
> No more firing was heard at Brussels

—the pursuit rolled miles away. The darkness came down on the field and city, and Amelia was praying for George, who was lying on his face, dead, with a bullet through his heart.

In the end, strategic errors by Napoleon and his generals and savage, fearless fighting by the coalition troops led to Napoleon's utter and final defeat. He was forced to give up the French throne a second time and was exiled to Saint Helena. King Louis XVIII was restored to the throne.

Vanity Fair is not the only work of literature to feature the Battle of Waterloo. British poet Lord Byron gives it an important place in *Childe Harold's Pilgrimage*, as does Thomas Hardy in *The Dynasts*. Among French writers, Victor Hugo includes the battle in *Les Misérables*.

Victorian England

The Victorian Age began in 1837 when eighteen-year-old Queen Victoria ascended to the British throne, and ended with her death in 1901. Victoria and her husband, Albert, set the tone of English life and culture for most of a century. It was a time of social and moral conservatism; the family values of the time were similar to those touted in late twentieth-century America. Pragmatism was valued above romance, duty above pleasure.

The early Victorian period was a time of social reforms. Laws were passed governing working conditions of women and children (they could not work in underground mines, for example), and attempts were made to improve conditions in prisons and insane asylums. Efforts to broaden access to education (England had no public schools at the time) stalled because of controversy over the Church of England's role in expanded education. Writers such as Thackeray and Charles Dickens took up the cause of reform, using their writing to point out the need for prison reforms and educational programs and to expose the evils of industrialization and the class system.

In the middle of the nineteenth century, England was experiencing unprecedented political, industrial, and economic power, fueled by the Industrial Revolution and by the wealth from the colonies. All forms of transportation boomed; railroad ridership increased sevenfold, and the ship industry grew. Living standards of the working class and middle class were buoyed, and trade unions were formed to promote the interests of skilled workers.

In the late 1850s, after unrest in India, the British government abolished the East India Company and took over direct rule of the subcontinent. Queen Victoria was declared Empress of India in 1876, and the empire continued to expand, especially in Asia and Africa.

Critical Overview

Vanity Fair was published in several installments beginning on January 1, 1847, and reviews soon began appearing in London's magazines. Most writers who reviewed the early segments were not enthusiastic, nor was the public. The primary complaints of both critics and readers were that the novel was progressing slowly and without much action and that all the characters were unlikable.

Reception turned positive, however, after the first four installments. Once the whole of *Vanity Fair* had been published, it sold well (one 1848 reviewer wrote, "Everybody, it is to be supposed, has read the volume by this time.") and earned many glowing reviews. George Henry Lewes wrote in *The Athenaeum*, For some years Mr. Thackeray has been a marked man in letters—but known rather as an amusing sketcher than as a serious artist. Light playful contributions to periodical literature and two amusing books of travel were insufficient to make a reputation; but a reputation he must now be held to have established by his *Vanity Fair*. It is his greatest effort and his greatest success.

In *Quarterly Review*, Elizabeth Rigby wrote,

> We were perfectly aware that Mr. Thackeray had of old assumed the jester's habit, in order the more unrestrainedly to indulge the

privilege of speaking the truth … but still we were little prepared for the keen observation, the deep wisdom, and the consummate art which he has interwoven in the slight texture and whimsical pattern of *Vanity Fair*.

Compare & Contrast

- **Early to Mid-Nineteenth Century:** People are routinely sent to prison when they are unable to pay their debts. Debtors' prisons are crowded, even during the relatively prosperous Victorian Age, and conditions are deplorable. Those who do not have family members or other benefactors to pay their debts sometimes spend years in prison. Charles Dickens and other authors write movingly of the plight of debtors, and reformers seek to abolish the prisons.

  Today: Debtors' prisons have been replaced by bankruptcy laws, which allow debtors to have most debts forgiven and to make a fresh financial start. Even during the economic boom of the 1990s, millions of individuals and small businesses declare bankruptcy.

- **Early to Mid-Nineteenth Century:**

Although the former American colonies have won their independence, the British Empire still spans the globe. India, explored and exploited by the British East India Company, is now completely under British rule and is the "jewel in the crown." Britain also has colonies in Africa, Indonesia, Australia and New Zealand, South America, Canada, and the Caribbean.

Today: What was once the British Empire is now the British Commonwealth, a collection of former colonies, most of which are independent nations, with formal ties to Britain. Among the Commonwealth nations are India, Canada, Australia, and New Zealand.

Charlotte Brontë was such an admirer of *Vanity Fair* that, on its merits, she dedicated the second edition of *Jane Eyre* to Thackeray, writing in her preface:

> I think I see in him an intellect profounder and more unique than his contemporaries have yet recognized … I think no commentator on his writings has yet found the

comparison that suits him, the terms which rightly characterise his talent.

Even an anonymous reviewer for *The London Review*, who felt that the meanness of the characters defeated the novel, acknowledged, "*Vanity Fair* is a remarkable book, brilliant, entertaining," before adding, "but if we plunge beneath the sparkling surface, it is a dreary book. It gives the real, and utterly omits the ideal."

John Forster wrote prophetically in *The Examiner*,

> *Vanity Fair* must be admitted to be one of the most original works of real genius that has of late been given to the world.... The very novelty of tone in the book impeded its first success; but it will be daily more justly appreciated; and will take a lasting place in our literature.

In his 1909 book *Studies in Several Literatures*, Harry Thurston Peck assessed the novel after sixty years. "*Vanity Fair* is one of the greatest books in English literature," he wrote, "but it belongs to purely English literature, and not to the great masterpieces which the whole world owns and to which it gives unforced admiration."

History has, to an extent, proven Forster and Peck correct. *Vanity Fair* is still read and admired but not as widely as the best work of Thackeray's contemporary Dickens. It is, however, Thackeray's most lasting work, the one that modern readers most enjoy. Robert A. Colby, in his introduction to a 1989 edition of *Vanity Fair*, wrote, We, it seems, are attracted to the very qualities that disturbed Thackeray's contemporaries—impersonality, cynicism, tough-mindedness. Indeed, its coruscating wit, ingenuity, and vivacious style continue to make *Vanity Fair* the most immediately attractive of Thackeray's novels to the general reader.

What Do I Read Next?

- *W. M. Thackeray Library*, edited by Richard Pearson and published in 1996, presents an array of Thackeray's writing, including short fiction and nonfiction, plus a full-length biography by Lewis Melville.

- *Jane Eyre*, by Charlotte Brontë, was published in 1847, the same year in which the first installments of *Vanity Fair* appeared. Brontë's novel has some similarities to Thackeray's in that the main character is an orphaned English governess who becomes romantically involved with her employer.

- *Wuthering Heights*, by Emily Brontë, also was published in 1847. Like *Vanity Fair*, it is considered one of the classics of Victorian literature. The novel is a story of romance and revenge.

- *Little Dorrit*, by Charles Dickens, was first published serially in 1857. Another Victorian classic, Dickens's book tells the story of Amy Dorrit, born in the debtors' prison where her father lives. Major themes are social class, financial reversals, and romance.

- *Far from the Madding Crowd*, by Thomas Hardy, was published serially in 1874 and also is ranked as a Victorian classic. It is the story of a female farmer and her three suitors. Virginia Woolf commented that this book "must hold its place among the great English novels." It has the distinction of being Hardy's only novel to offer readers a happy ending.

- *Red, Red Rose*, by Marjorie Farrell, was published in 1999. It tells the story of Val Aston, the illegitimate son of an English earl who becomes an officer in the English army during the Napoleonic wars. Aston is noble in character if not by birth, yet his social standing is an obstacle to his marrying the woman he loves.

Sources

Bronté, Charlotte, Preface to *Jane Eyre*, Clarendon Press, 1969.

Colby, Robert A., "Historical Introduction," in *Vanity Fair*, Garland, 1989, pp. 632-37.

Cuddon, J. A., *The Penguin Dictionary of Literary Terms and Literary Theory*, Penguin Books, 1992, pp. 827-32.

Forster, John, *Examiner*, No. 2112, July 22, 1848, pp. 468-70.

Karlson, Marilyn Naufftus, "William Makepeace Thackeray," in *Dictionary of Literary Biography*, Volume 55: *Victorian Prose Writers Before 1867*, edited by William B. Thesing, Gale Research, 1987, pp. 303-14.

Lewes, George Henry, *Athenaeum*, No. 1085, August 12, 1848, pp. 794-97.

Peck, Harry Thurston, *Studies in Several Literatures*, Dodd, Mead and Company, 1909, pp. 149-61.

Ray, Gordon N., ed., *The Letters and Private Papers of William Makepeace Thackeray*, Vol. 2, Harvard University Press, 1945–1946, p. 309.

Review of *Vanity Fair*, in *London Review*, Vol. XVI, No. XXXII, July 1861, pp. 291-94.

Rigby, Elizabeth, Review of *Vanity Fair*, in

Quarterly Review, December 1848, pp. 155-62.

"William Makepeace Thackeray: *Vanity Fair: A Novel without a Hero*," in *Characters in Nineteenth-Century Literature*, Gale Research, 1993, pp. 490-96.

Further Reading

Mitchell, Sally, *Daily Life in Victorian England*, Greenwood Publishing Group, 1996.

This comprehensive look at both city and country life in Victorian England covers social classes, morals, economics and finance, laws, and more. It includes illustrations and excerpts from primary source documents.

Pascoe, David, ed., *Selected Journalism 1850–1870*, Penguin USA, 1998.

This generous collection of the journalistic writings of Charles Dickens offers minute and gritty details of life in London in the mid-nineteenth century.

Peters, Catherine, *Thackeray: A Writer's Life*, Sutton Publishing, 2000.

This recent biography examines Thackeray's life and how his writing was influenced by his experiences and the world around him.

Thackeray, William Makepeace, *Thackerayana*, Haskell House, 1970.

This is an engaging, self-illustrated collection of anecdotes and observations, many of them humorous, about everything from Thackeray's childhood to his favorite literary characters.

Lightning Source UK Ltd.
Milton Keynes UK
UKHW020632201119
353895UK00013B/990/P